# About the authors

Aidan Dunlea BComm ACA is Manager – General Practice in the Cork office of KPMG Stokes Kennedy Crowley.

Niall MacLochlainn BComm FCA is financial manager for Mitsui Denman (Ireland) Limited. He lectures in financial and management accounting to students taking their final professional accounting examinations and is Secretary of both the Cork and Munster Societies of Chartered Accountants.

# AUDITING STANDARDS
## A quick reference

**Aidan Dunlea and**
**Niall MacLochlainn**

Oak Tree Press

Dublin and London

Published by Oak Tree Press, Dublin and London.



A catalogue record for this book is available from the British Library.

ISBN 1-872853-95-1.



Printed in Ireland by Colour Books, Dublin.

# Contents

* + SAS 460 Nov 1995
(Change to FRS 8)

# Introduction

This book is intended as a companion volume to ***Accounting Standards: A quick reference*** (see inside back cover) and has been developed with the same objectives in mind.

Students of auditing will find it useful as an initial introduction to auditing standards, as well as a convenient means of revising the great bulk of material they contain.

Practitioners will find it useful as a reminder of the obscure (and perhaps not so obscure) points that crop in the day-to-day practice of auditing – and as a means of updating their knowledge on the many recent developments in auditing, in particular the issue of revised auditing standards following the completion of the Auditing Practices Board's Revisions Project. We hope that the Application Notes will prove useful to practitioners in implementing the key points required by the standards.

Our aim – as suggested by the title – is to provide a quick and easy work of reference, one that readers will find both comprehensive and concise. Thus, all standards in force in issue at 31 March 1995 are included.

The contents are up-to-date at the time of going to press. As auditing standards are continually developing, further editions will be published from time to time to ensure that readers are kept abreast of developments.

Your comments and suggestions to improve the value of this book to its users are welcome.

**Aidan Dunlea**
**Niall MacLochlainn**
**April 1995**

# The development of Auditing Standards

The development of formal auditing standards and guidelines began with the formation of the Auditing Practices Committee (APC) in 1976.

## Auditing Practices Committee

APC was established by the Consultative Committee of Accountancy Bodies (CCAB), which comprises the six principal accountancy bodies in the United Kingdom and Ireland:

- The Chartered Association of Certified Accountants
- The Chartered Institute of Management Accountants
- The Chartered Institute of Public Finance and Accountancy
- The Institute of Chartered Accountants in England and Wales
- The Institute of Chartered Accountants in Ireland
- The Institute of Chartered Accountants of Scotland.

APC developed almost 50 pronouncements relating to the audit of entities, covering topics as diverse as:

- Reporting to shareholders and management
- Procedures to be undertaken in specific circumstances
- Guidance for particular sectors and industries and in operational circumstances.

Throughout, the basis of the auditor's work was the statutory duty set out in company law.

## Auditing Practices Board

Because of rapid changes in the business world and the increasing demands of users of financial statements, a new body, the Auditing Practices Board (APB), was set up in 1991 by CCAB. This new board differs from its predecessor in that its voting membership is evenly divided between practising auditors and user representatives (including nominees of the Bank of England, the London Stock Exchange, the National Audit Office, the Audit Commission, the Securities and Investments Board, the UK Department of Trade and Industry, and the Irish Department of Enterprise and Employment).

APB's stated objectives are:

- To establish high standards in auditing
- To meet the developing needs of users of financial information
- To ensure there is public confidence in the audit process.

The concerns and perceptions of the auditing process as expressed by a (limited) survey of users of financial statements was set out in APB's paper *The Future Development of Auditing* (November 1992) and included:

**Role and scope of the audit:**

- Auditors should also recognise that there are other interest groups – not just shareholders
- Auditors should be concerned with directors' stewardship, future prospects and risks (not just the historical aspect of financial statements), detection of fraud and the effectiveness of internal controls

**Independence:**

- A perception that auditors are not sufficiently independent

**Audit report:**

- A perception that audit reports are not informative enough, do not set out major findings, or issues or concerns raised during the audit

**Competition:**

- Audit standards may have been lowered in order to match competitors' (lower) fees

**Litigation:**

- Well-publicised legal cases against auditors act as a barrier to audit innovation

**Regulation:**

- A perception that the audit regulation system was not effective (It was not clear to APB whether those surveyed were aware of the changes recently made on the implementation of the EU Eighth Directive – see section on the legal framework for the new rules)

**Skills:**

- A greater need for continuous training and development of auditors (to meet the changing needs of users).

## Future developments

Following consultation on the 1992 paper, APB issued *The Audit Agenda* (December 1994), which proposes a framework for the future development of auditing. Its proposals include:

- Extending the scope of listed company audits
- Differentiating between the audit of listed companies and owner-managed businesses
- Developing specific responsibilities for audit committees of listed companies
- Tougher penalties for directors and staff who deceive auditors.

## Pronouncements

APB's pronouncements fall into three main categories:

- Statements of Auditing Standards (SASs)
- Practice Notes
- Bulletins.

There are also consultative documents, research documents and other documents of general interest issued on both auditing and related services.

Proposed auditing standards are issued in draft form for comment and sometimes reissued again as a draft in the light of the arguments expressed. Before a draft statement becomes a full standard, it must be approved by at least 75 per cent of the voting members of APB.

## Compliance

Compliance with the basic principles and essential procedures in Auditing Standards is mandatory for all auditors. Explanatory and other material in the standards provide an aid to interpretation.

Practice Notes, Bulletins, consultative documents and research documents indicate APB's view of the correct procedures to be followed but are not mandatory.

Auditing Standards use words like **plan, design, assess, consider.** In practice, the auditor must decide, using his or her professional judgement, the meaning of these words as they relate to each client. In the event of litigation, the auditor must be able to justify the original judgement. Good documentation (a requirement of the standards) is clearly imperative!

## Effective date for implementation of Auditing Standards

Most of the Auditing Standards (SASs) come into effect for audits of financial statements for periods ending on or after 23 December 1995.

The effective dates for the others are:

| | |
|---|---|
| SAS 100 | 30 June 1995 |
| SAS 120 | 30 June 1995 |
| SAS 130 | 30 June 1995 |
| SAS 600 | 30 September 1993 |
| SAS 620 | 1 May 1994. |

# Auditing – the legal framework

The Eighth Directive of the European Community (now the European Union) was enacted into UK law by the 1989 Companies Act (in Ireland, by the 1990 Companies Act).

As a result, the law now sets out specific rules on the following matters:

- Qualification for appointment as auditor
- Resignation of an auditor
- Removal of an auditor
- Registration of auditors
- Auditors' rights (and duties) relating to books of account
- Auditors' rights to attend and be heard at general meetings
- Penalties for making false statements to auditors.

## Qualification for appointment as auditor

To qualify as an auditor, an individual must be a member of one of the Recognised Supervisory Bodies (RSBs) and be eligible under its rules to practice as an auditor.

In the case of a partnership or incorporated practice, the individuals responsible for the conduct of audit work ('responsible individuals') must be qualified members of an RSBs. Where the partnership contains unqualified partners, these persons must become affiliates or regulated non-members of the RSB. Control of the partnership (75 per cent of voting rights) must be held by qualified individuals or registered auditors.

In the UK, the RSBs are recognised by order of the Department of Trade and Industry or the Department of Economic

Development (Northern Ireland). In Ireland, RSBs are recognised by the Department of Enterprise and Employment.

To be recognised as an RSB, an accounting body must have rules to ensure that its members:

- Conduct their work with professional integrity
- Comply with technical standards
- Remain competent
- Are independent of their clients.

In addition, an RSB must have provisions relating to disciplinary procedures – that is, investigation of complaints against members, admission and expulsion of members, suspension, or withdrawal of practising certificate etc.

The legislation also specifies those who are ineligible to act as auditors. These are persons closely connected with the audited entity, such as:

- An officer or servant
- A person who was an officer or servant within the period to which the audit related
- A close relation of an officer
- A partner of, or someone employed by, an officer
- A person disqualified as auditor of a group company.

Note: A body corporate is not permitted to conduct audits of companies registered under legislation in the Republic of Ireland.

## Resignation of an auditor

If an auditor of a limited company wishes to resign, or does not wish to be re-appointed, he or she must:

- Notify the company in writing
- Include a statement that there are no circumstances which he or she believes should be brought to the notice of the members or creditors of the company

- Send a copy of the notice to the company (in Ireland, he or she must also notify the Registrar of Companies within 14 days).

If there are circumstances that the auditor believes should be brought to the notice of members or creditors, the company must:

- Send a copy of the auditor's notice to every person entitled to receive a copy of the accounts
- Convene an extraordinary general meeting, if requested by the auditor
- Circulate a further statement from the auditor regarding the circumstances connected with the resignation, if requested.

## Removal of an auditor

Extended notice (28 days, instead of the normal 21 days for an ordinary resolution) is required where a limited company proposes to remove an auditor, or to appoint another instead, at the AGM.

The company must notify the present auditor, who is entitled to attend and be heard at the general meeting on any part of the business that concerns him as former auditor.

## Registration of auditors

Details of all those qualified for appointment as auditor are available for public inspection. In the UK, the list is maintained by the RSBs; in Ireland, the list is available for inspection at the Companies Registration Office, Dublin Castle).

## Auditor's rights (and duties) relating to books of account

The auditor is entitled to:

- Right of access at all reasonable times to the books, accounts and vouchers of the company
- Request any employee of the company for such information and explanations considered necessary for the performance of the duties of the audit
- Request information from subsidiary companies and their auditors.

If an auditor forms an opinion, at any time, that proper books of account are not being kept by the company, he or she must serve notice on the entity stating his or her opinion (and, if the position is not rectified within seven days, must notify the Registrar of Companies).

## Auditor's rights relating to general meetings

The auditor:

- Is entitled to receive all notices of all general meetings
- Is entitled to be heard at the meetings
- Must read the auditors' report at annual general meetings of the company.

## Penalties for making false statements to auditors

It is a criminal offence for an employee of a company to knowingly or recklessly give a misleading, false or deceptive statement to an auditor.

# Statements of Auditing Standards (at 31 March 1995)

## Evidence

400 Audit evidence
410 Analytical procedures
420 Audit of accounting estimates
430 Audit sampling
440 Management representations
450 Opening balances and comparatives
460 Related parties (draft)
470 Overall review of financial statements

## Using the work of others

500 Considering the work of internal audit
510 The relationship between principal auditors and other auditors
520 Using the work of an expert

## Reporting

600 Auditors' report on financial statements
610 Reports to directors or management
620 The auditors' right and duty to report to regulators in the financial sector

## Engagements other than audits of financial statements

Statement of Standards for Reporting Accountants – 'Audit Exemption Reports'

## Particular industries and sectors

No standards issued

# SAS 010
# *The scope and authority of APB pronouncements*

**Issued May 1993**


## Summary
Sets out the principal categories of pronouncements of the Auditing Practices Board (APB), the distinctions between them, and the authority of each.


## Key Points
Pronouncements of the APB include:

- Statements of Auditing Standards (SASs)
- Practice Notes
- Bulletins
- Other documents

*SASs*

Auditors must comply with Basic Principles when auditing financial statements (mandatory).

Only apply SASs to material items.

SASs include explanatory and other material to assist interpretation of basic principles (this material is not mandatory).

Apparent failure to comply with SASs could result in disciplinary or regulatory action being taken against an auditor (practising certificate could be suspended or revoked).

SASs are likely to be used in a court of law as evidence of the standard of work required of an auditor.

SASs comply, where possible, with equivalent standards set out by the International Auditing Practices Committee.

*Practice Notes*
These set out how to apply SASs to particular circumstances and/or industries (persuasive but not mandatory)

*Bulletins*
Guidance on new or emerging issues (persuasive but not mandatory).

*Other documents*
Consultative documents, research studies etc. to stimulate debate and interest in the auditing process.

# SAS 100
## *Objective and general principles governing an audit of financial statements*

**Issued March 1995**

### Summary
Sets out the objectives and principles governing audits of financial statements.

### Key Points
Auditors must:

- Comply with auditing standards as set out in Statements of Auditing Standards (SASs)
- Design procedures to obtain sufficient evidence that financial statements:
  > Contain no material misstatement
  > Are prepared in accordance with accounting standards and company law
- Issue an audit report setting out a clear opinion
- Comply with ethical principles (integrity; objectivity; independence; professional competence and behaviour; confidentiality).

The management of an entity is responsible for the preparation and presentation of financial statements.

### Application Notes
Inform client in writing (prior to commencement of the audit) of the basis of fees charged for the services provided.

Ensure that the client has full and complete understanding of:

- Services to be covered by the fee
- Basis of fees charged for present and for future years (important when competitive quote is requested).

Be able to demonstrate that SASs were followed and that the client understands the fee basis if a very low fee level is quoted.

Auditors may exercise a lien on certain books and papers of a client in respect of unpaid fees. However the auditor should take reasonable steps to resolve any such dispute before exercising a lien.

Regularly review the ethical guidelines set out by the relevant RSB and ensure compliance with same.

Regularly review the guidelines on maintaining competence (recruitment, training policies) issued by the RSBs.

Design procedures to ensure that all audits are conducted in accordance with SASs. Monitor compliance with audit regulations (termed 'internal monitoring'/'quality assurance'/'audit compliance') on a regular basis – sample audit files annually.

Design procedures to ensure that all financial statements are prepared in accordance with relevant financial reporting standards and legislation.

# SAS 110
## *Fraud and error*

**Issued January 1995**


### Summary
Sets out standards required of, and gives guidance to, auditors when considering the possibility of fraud and/or error in financial statements.


### Key Points
Directors have a responsibility to prevent and detect fraud or error by developing proper accounting and internal control systems.

Auditors must assess the risk of material errors in the financial statements due to fraud or unintentional mistakes.

Design audit procedures to reasonably detect material misstatements in the financial statements.

Fraud is often difficult to detect. If misstatement is suspected, perform additional procedures. Document the nature, circumstances and possible effect of suspected fraud or error.

If a suspicion of error persists, discuss it with (the appropriate level of) management, directors or audit committee.

If a material error is found, disclose it immediately to management, the board of directors, or audit committee. Consider the implications of the material error on the accounts, management representations, other audit procedures performed and the audit report.

Auditors may have to report suspected case of fraud (or error) to third parties by law (refer to SAS 620) or in 'public interest cases' (because of potential breach of confidentiality, which can only be justified in exceptional circumstances, auditors should obtain legal advice to ensure that qualified privilege is retained).

The requirements of this SAS apply to all activities of the entity – including those carried on abroad.

## Application Notes

At the audit planning stage, consider whether any of the following circumstances apply (which increase the risk of error) and plan the audit accordingly:

- Competence of management is in query
- Failure in internal controls
- High turnover of key accounting personnel
- Major understaffing in the finance department
- Pressures within the operation (for example, short life products needing major investment; changes in customer mix or their credit terms; lack of working capital; very severe accounting deadlines)
- Unusual transactions, especially near the year end, that have a major impact on the results
- Where sufficient audit evidence is not obtained or is difficult to obtain
- Transactions with related parties
- Management has not acted on weaknesses in internal control pointed out in previous management letters.

Discuss with management the procedures in place for detecting and preventing fraud or error. Suggest improvements if weaknesses are noted.

Ensure the letter of engagement establishes the responsibility of management to prevent and detect fraud and error.

In a group situation, ensure that auditors of subsidiaries (including foreign components) conduct their audits in accordance with this SAS.

Where audit procedures indicate the likely occurrence of fraud or error, perform additional or modified audit procedures. Report instances of fraud or error to management, directors or audit committee (as appropriate).

Consider the implications of fraud or error detected during the audit, particularly on the validity of management representations.

If fraud or error is detected, ensure it is properly disclosed and/or accounted for in the financial statements. Even if corrected, it may be necessary to qualify the audit report.

Consider the need for legal advice if fraud or error is detected. In extreme cases , there may be a need to make disclosure to a proper authority. Consider the conflict between client confidentiality and public interest.

Obtain written confirmation from directors that the financial statements contain no material misstatements caused by fraud or error.

In exceptional cases, consider withdrawal from audit engagement.

## Definitions

*Fraud*

The use of deception to obtain an unjust or illegal financial advantage, or intentional misrepresentations.

*Error*

An unintentional mistake in financial statements.

# SAS 120
# *Consideration of law and regulations*

**Issued January 1995**

## Summary

Sets out the responsibility of auditors to consider the effect on the financial statements of non-compliance with the laws and regulations an entity is operating under.

## Key Points

Directors are responsible for compliance with the various laws and regulations affecting the business, both in the home market and abroad.

Auditors must ensure that the financial statements are prepared in conformity with the relevant laws and regulations (primary responsibility).

Auditors must obtain a general understanding of the statutory framework of the business operations. Develop procedures for this.

Obtain from the directors written confirmation of all possible non-compliance, including the consequences of same. Read correspondence between the entity and the appropriate authorities. If there is no non-compliance, the auditor need not investigate further.

If non-compliance is admitted by the directors or becomes known during the audit, discuss it with the directors. Reconsider (if appropriate) the assessment of audit risk and the reliability of audit evidence.

Auditors have a responsibility to qualify their report to shareholders if non-compliance has had a material effect on the financial statements (where there is incorrect accounting treatment or inadequate disclosure).

In certain cases, auditors may have to report non-compliance to third parties (for example, regulatory authorities).

## Application Notes

For each client, list (in the permanent audit file) the particular laws and regulations applicable to the entity. These may apply to the entity as a whole, or to certain sections or products. Update this list each year.

Keep an abstract of the key regulations. Confirm each year that no change has occurred (amend if applicable).

Ensure that management understands its obligation to comply with laws and regulations governing both the preparation of financial statements and the environment within which the entity conducts its business. Include a note to this effect in the engagement letter.

Check:

- Whether the client has procedures to ensure that new regulations are notified to those responsible in the entity
- Whether the client has procedures for monitoring compliance with laws and reporting breaches of regulations
- What action has been taken when breaches in regulations were reported.

Read the correspondence files between the entity and the appropriate authorities. Consider whether a letter directly from the relevant authority is required to confirm the situation.

Ensure that the audit team is aware of any statutory requirement to report the entity's compliance with specific laws or regulations to a third party (see SAS 620).

In the letter of representation, obtain confirmation from the directors that they have disclosed all possible non-compliance, and actual or contingent consequences arising therefrom.

Consider the impact of any non-compliance on audit risk and the validity of management representations.

Report instances of non-compliance to management, directors or audit committee, as appropriate.

Report instances of material non-compliance to the addressees of audit report (see SAS 600).

Consider the need to disclose any breaches in compliance to the proper authority in the public interest. Obtain legal advice before doing so, if necessary.

In a group situation, ensure that the auditors of subsidiaries (including foreign components) also apply appropriate procedures.

In exceptional cases, consider withdrawal from the audit engagement.

## Comment

With many new EU directives being issued each year, it is important that the client (and the auditor) has procedures in place to learn about new legislation. Some legislation is of general application – for example, health and safety (VDUs, and manual handling) – but some are specific to one industry – for example, the requirement for package tour operators to provide security for passengers' deposits.

# SAS 130
# *The going concern basis in financial statements*

**Issued November 1994**


## Summary

Sets out standards for auditors in assessing whether the going concern concept should be used (and the basis adequately disclosed) in the financial statements.


## Key Points

Applies to all audits intended to give a true and fair view.

The directors must satisfy themselves, by considering the entity's future, that the going concern concept is appropriate in preparing the financial statements and that the Notes to the financial statements contain relevant disclosures where necessary.

Where the directors do not attempt to satisfy themselves adequately, this constitutes a limitation of audit scope.

The auditor must **plan** the audit and **design** audit procedures to identify material matters in the period that directors have considered that could impact on the going concern concept.

The future period for assessing going concern is not specified – and will thus depend on each entity's circumstances – but a guideline of one year from the accounts approval date is indicated.

If a short period (less than one year ahead) is chosen by the directors, they will have to decide whether to include additional disclosures explaining the assumptions in the financial statements. The auditor must **consider** whether these disclosures are adequate.

If the directors' disclosures are not adequate, include the necessary further disclosures as part of the audit opinion (qualification of the audit opinion is not required on the basis of non-disclosure alone).

If the auditor has a significant worry about the appropriateness of the going concern basis, include a explanatory paragraph in the audit report but do **not** qualify.

The auditor must **discuss** with the directors the future viability of the entity and consider whether written representations from the directors are required.

If written representations are requested and not given, **consider**:

- Why representations not given
- Whether this constitutes a limitation on audit scope (if so, qualify audit opinion).

If the auditor **disagrees** that the going concern basis is appropriate, he or she should give an **adverse** audit opinion. Inform the directors that they should obtain legal advice on the implications of trading while the entity is (or may be) insolvent.

Examine cash flow forecasts, the extent of borrowing facilities, the amount and pattern of supplier credit, and the directors' plans for the business (look at key assumptions used, apply sensitivity analysis, and assess bankers' intentions regarding facilities). Discussion with the directors regarding future plans may be sufficient to satisfy the auditor that a period of one year from the accounts approval date has been examined by the directors in assessing the appropriateness of the going concern basis.

Apply SAS 130 to group accounts, even though one or more subsidiaries' accounts may not be prepared on a going concern basis.

## Application Notes

At the audit planning stage, perform a preliminary assessment of the appropriateness of the going concern basis for the preparation of financial statements – discuss with the directors.

Consider the period chosen by the directors in assessing whether the entity is a going concern – is it reasonable and does it have regard to the foreseeable future.

Check whether management has systems in place to identify future uncertainties affecting going concern (for example, projected sales, profits, cash flow statements). Suggest improvements if weaknesses are noted.

Consider whether any of the following apply:

- Substantial sales of fixed assets (not being replaced)
- Major restructuring of debt
- Legal restrictions on operations (in any market)
- Obsolescence of a key product due to technology
- Loss of major customers, suppliers, or management staff
- Depressed markets, where the company is heavily dependent on a few products
- Excess of liabilities over assets
- Cash flow problems – inability to pay creditors on due dates/difficulties in keeping within bank facility limits
- Defaults on loan agreements
- Significant operating losses
- Shortage of important supplies, or labour difficulties.

This list is not all-inclusive, nor does the existence of one or more of the above always signify a going concern issue. Other factors may lessen the significance of these indicators.

Review cash flow, results and other forecasts for at least one year (normally) from audit completion date. Examine significant assumptions for reasonableness.

If the directors have chosen a period of less than one year from approval date of the financial statements for the assessment of going concern, perform the above tests for the period and ensure the reasons for the choice of period are given in the financial statements.

In a smaller entity, discussion with directors regarding future plans and information relating to business trends may be sufficient – summarise the discussions.

Audit staff should immediately report any matters indicating going concern difficulties to the audit partner for discussion with the directors.

Consider the implications of going concern matters for the financial statements, including situations where another basis of accounting has been used.

Ensure that appropriate references to matters that may impact on the going concern basis are included in the letter of representation (which should be dated as close as possible to the date of signing the audit report).

In a group situation, consider whether the qualification of a subsidiary's accounts on a going concern basis has an impact on the consolidated statements.

# SAS 140
# *Engagement letters*

**Issued March 1995**

## Summary

Sets out requirements for engagement letters – both the content of a letter and its communication to the client.

## Key Points

Auditors should agree in writing the terms of the engagement with each new client.

SAS applies also to other services such as tax, accounting, management consultancy.

Update the engagement letter where necessary (if not necessary, remind client of the original letter) – for example, where there is new management, new owners, or a change of business.

If asked to change the terms of the engagement before it is completed:

- If appropriate, update the engagement letter
- If not appropriate, consider position – take legal advice, if necessary.

## Application Notes

Issue an engagement letter to each audit client.

Reissue the engagement letter at least every three years.

Revise the engagement letter immediately each time there is a major change in key personnel, new directors, owners, or in client's business.

Confirm the terms of engagement annually with client when a new letter is not issued.

Tailor the engagement letter for each client's circumstances, requirements, etc. (although they will have common headings).

Issue a separate engagement letter where services other than audit (for example, taxation, accounting, investment business advice, etc.) are being given.

In joint audits, confirm the respective responsibilities of the participating firms and issue a joint letter of engagement. Consider the need for separate engagement letters for subsidiaries or other segments of the entity.

*Contents of engagement letters*

- Summary of responsibilities of directors and auditors
- Scope of the engagement
- Form of any reports
- Confirmation of acceptance by the auditor
- Fees, billing – agreed fee and payment terms (or basis of billing)
- Reference to other engagements between auditor and client
- Timetable for the engagement
- Involvement of internal auditors, other auditors or experts
- List the work the client is to do and expected date of completion
- Request details of stocktaking arrangements, locations, times, etc.

- Procedures to be followed in the event of complaint (required automatically by some professional bodies).

The statement of responsibilities of the directors should refer to:

- Preparation of financial statements which give a true and fair view
- Keeping proper accounting records and safeguarding the assets of the entity (statutory duties)
- Preventing and detecting fraud and error (SAS 110)
- Compliance with laws and regulations affecting the entity (SAS 120)
- Selecting suitable accounting policies and applying them consistently
- Making estimates and judgements that are reasonable and prudent
- Preparation of financial statements on a going concern basis – unless it is not appropriate (SAS 130)
- Giving all information and explanations required by the auditors, including events post balance sheet.

# SAS 150
## *Subsequent events*

**Issued March 1995**

### Summary
Sets out the standards required in assessing the impact of events occurring after the balance sheet date up to the time the financial statements are put before the members for approval.

### Key Points
Three stages to be considered:

- From end of the accounting period to the date of the audit report
- From the date of the audit report to the issue of the financial statements
- After the financial statements have been issued but before they are laid before the members.

*Stage 1*
Design audit procedures to ensure that all material post balance sheet events to the date of the audit report are treated correctly in the financial statements (refer to SSAP 17 *Post balance sheet events*).

*Stage 2*
There is no responsibility to perform audit procedures or make enquiries. But if the auditor becomes aware of material events affecting the financial statements, the choices are:

- To issue a new audit report on amended financial statements

- To issue a qualified report (assuming none issued to date), where the directors do not amend the financial statements
- To request management not to issue financial statements to members (or anyone else). If financial statements are issued, the auditor should consider making a statement at the entity's AGM and also consider his or her position as auditor.

*Stage 3*
There is no responsibility on the auditor to make enquiries. But if the auditor becomes aware of material events which, if known during the audit, might have resulted in a different audit report, he or she should discuss them with the directors and consider the implications.

If amended financial statements are issued, a new audit report is required. This must:

- Include an explanatory paragraph regarding the change (or refer to a new Note in the financial statements which should set out the reason)
- Refer to the earlier report
- Be newly dated.

Ensure that management informs those who received a copy of earlier financial statements of the new situation.

## Application Notes

Perform the review of subsequent events as near as possible to the date of signing the audit report.

Review minutes of meetings of directors, management, audit committee, etc. post year end.

Compare actual results for the new financial year against budget. Make enquiries if major variances are arising.

Note details of any new financing arranged, the outcome of review of banking facilities, etc.

Review the cash flow post year end. Note any unusual payments or receipts.

Arrange for auditors of other subsidiaries or associates of the entity to notify the principal auditor of important issues affecting their audit.

While discussing the final draft of the accounts, enquire of management whether any subsequent event has occurred.

Request management to inform the auditor of significant events arising after the accounts have been approved by the directors (and the audit report issued) but before the accounts have been approved by the shareholders.

Refer to APB Practice Notes, if revised financial statements are issued.

Consider changes in legislation, and enquiries, reviews or reports by regulatory bodies.

Review the outcome of areas of significant judgement, including accounting estimates, and litigation.

Perform an up-to-date review of material matters highlighted during the the course of the audit field work.

Obtain written representations from management about post balance sheet events (SAS 440).

# SAS 160
# *Other information in documents containing audited financial statements*

**Issued March 1995**


### Summary
Requires the auditor to consider the contents of other documents in the annual report of an entity before signing the audit report.


### Key Points
Other information includes the directors' report (a legal requirement), the operating and financial review, the chairman's report, employment data, five year summaries, and ratios.

Auditors have a statutory responsibility to check that there are no inconsistencies between the financial statements and the directors' report. If there are, the audit report must refer to the inconsistencies.

Discuss any inconsistency between the financial statements and incorrectly presented data in 'other information' with the directors. The objective should be to amend the 'other information'. If amended, no further action is required.

If not amended, consider:

- Whether the financial statements give a true and fair view(and the audit report implications if they do not) or

- Whether, if the financial statements do give a true and fair view, the auditor can continue with the audit engagement (consider resigning).

## Application Notes

Near audit completion time, obtain and read the entire package that will contain the audited financial statements.

Request management to give the final package to the auditor for inspection before issue to the members of the entity.

Refer to any inconsistency between information in the directors' report and the financial statements in the audit report (statutory duty).

Consider whether there are any material inconsistencies (for example, do the statements in the operating and financial review really reflect the events of the year? Are graphs of selected information scaled fairly?). Discuss with management, directors or audit committee (as appropriate) with the objective of changing the 'other information'. Consider implications if corrective action is not taken. In extreme cases, consider withdrawal from the engagement.

# SAS 200
# *Planning*

**Issued March 1995**

## Summary

Gives guidance, in the context of recurring audits, on planning an audit.

## Key Points

Plan to ensure that the audit is performed effectively, efficiently, and in a timely manner.

Document the overall audit plan for the assignment.

Matters to be documented include:

- Knowledge of the entity's business
- Risk and materiality
- Nature, timing and extent of procedures
- Co-ordination, direction, supervision and review
- Other matters (for example, terms of the engagement, nature and timing of reports, etc.).

Document an audit programme, which is both a set of instructions to those involved and a means of controlling the recording and correct completion of work.

Change the audit plan and programme during the audit if conditions change or there are unexpected test results.

## Application Notes

Identify the critical audit areas and also the potential audit issues.

Perform analytical procedures.

Meet with management to discuss the engagement and to confirm preliminary results arising out of analytical procedures.

Discuss with management business issues, recent and future trend developments, changes in regulatory framework, etc. affecting the business.

If there is an internal audit team, consider how this will assist in the audit.

Consider the effect of related parties.

Decide whether the internal control systems are going to be relied on or whether more independent substantive evidence is required.

Consider using computer aided audit techniques (CAAT), if appropriate.

Examine the financial position of the entity.

Document the planning decisions and the intended scope and conduct of the audit in an overall audit plan.

Document an audit programme to achieve the objectives of the overall audit plan. Review the programme during the audit and, if unexpected results arise from audit procedures, revise the programme.

Set out a time plan for the audit, including:

- Stocktaking dates
- Audit start date
- Time to be spent in each audit area
- Contents of client's prepared schedules (and date expected)

- Review date(s)
- Client approval date.

If a group is involved, set out requirements for auditors of subsidiaries, including:
- Accounts completion dates
- Obtaining copies of reports to management, etc.

Assign staff appropriate to the risk levels and difficulties expected.

Consider the use of specialists on the audit engagement (for example, taxation experts, computer auditors, property valuers, etc.).

The audit partner should approve the audit plan and any revisions thereto.

# SAS 210
## *Knowledge of the business*

**Issued March 1995**

### Summary
Sets out the standards required of an audit team in obtaining sufficient knowledge of the client's business to be able to undertake the audit effectively.

### Key Points
In order to perform an audit of an entity to the highest standards, those involved must understand the business's operations, the industry(ies) involved and the markets for the products.

Accept an audit engagement only if one has sufficient knowledge to do a proper audit (either prior knowledge or easily obtainable subsequent knowledge).

At (or before ) each following audit, update knowledge levels, identify major changes and re-assess audit procedures.

The audit partner must ensure audit staff have sufficient knowledge of the client's business and that any new information that becomes available to any audit staff is passed on to all the audit team.

Consider whether the financial statements are consistent with the audit team's knowledge of the business.

Knowledge requirements:

- General economic factors:
  > Interest rates
  > Finance availability

> Inflation
> Tariffs
> Trade restrictions

- The industry:
  > Markets
  > Competition
  > Business risk
  > Adverse conditions
  > Key ratios/statistics
  > Accounting practices and problems
  > Environmental considerations
- The entity's management:
  > Structures – corporate, capital, and organisational
  > Management objectives, and philosophy
  > Board of directors
  > Internal audit experience
  > Incentive payments
  > Pressures
- The entity's business:
  > Products
  > Markets
  > Suppliers
  > Expenses
  > Research and development
  > Inventories and locations
  > Foreign exchange – assets, liabilities, transactions, hedging
- Financial performance factors:
  > Ratios
  > Trends
- Reporting environment:
  > Law
  > Statements of Auditing Standards
  > Financial Reporting Standards
  > Users' requirements.

## Application Notes

Have a permanent audit file for all audit clients. In this file, keep information to enable any audit team member to readily meet the 'knowledge requirements' of this SAS and to use for analytical procedure purposes (SAS 410). Keep the information as concise as possible. Maintain separate files for tax, audit, secretarial, correspondence. Make sure to update files each year (review at the end of the audit)

Meet clients regularly. At the audit planning stage, identify any significant changes in the business.

The audit partner should brief the audit team on developments in client's industry and business.

*Suggested contents of a permanent audit file*

- Summary of key financial ratios (historical record)
- List of main shareholdings
- List of directors, directors' shareholdings and options
- Brief notes on directors' experience, qualifications
- List of related parties
- Treasury policy and effect of exchange rates
- Sources of finance – summary of terms of loans and any special conditions or covenants
- Summary of critical accounting policies
- Summary of key risks and opportunities in the business
- Location of entity's premises, facilities, etc.
- Summary of key legislation and regulations affecting the entity
- Organisational chart(s) and job descriptions of key staff
- Summary of corporate objectives and management's policies and procedures to achieve same
- Summary of key products, services, market shares, etc.
- Copy of latest letter of engagement (SAS 140)
- Copy of last year's report to directors/management (SAS 610)

- Location of deeds of title to properties etc.
- Copies of latest valuations of properties, etc..
- Summary of any complex transactions undertaken by entity (for example, factoring, consignment stocks, securitisation, etc..)
- Summary of goodwill arising on each acquisition
- Summary of the information systems in use (SAS 310).

# SAS 220
# *Materiality and the audit*

**Issued March 1995**

## Summary

Gives guidance on the term 'materiality', which affects both auditing and financial reporting.

## Key Points

Materiality cannot be mathematically defined; it has both qualitative and quantitative aspects.

If the omission of a matter from (or an error in) the financial statements of an entity would influence a decision of one of the members, it is material.

Consider materiality when deciding on the design of audit procedures (preliminary assessment). Reconsider if test results indicate that the original assessment was incorrect.

Legal and regulatory requirements influence the materiality aspect of certain matters (for example, disclosure of directors' emoluments).

Consider materiality of total errors (specific errors found plus best estimate of projected errors) that have not been corrected in deciding whether the true and fair view is affected.

## Application Notes

At audit planning stage, perform a preliminary assessment of materiality in relation to the financial statements .

Document the assessment of materiality and planned audit approach in audit plan. Ensure audit partner approval is obtained.

Keep a summary sheet in the audit file and note the effect of all errors found.

Consider the items on this summary sheet in the context of the overall effect on the results, balance sheet, and on particular items such as payroll costs, directors' remuneration, etc.

Estimate the effect of other possible errors not found and assess the implications (quantification is more reliable if statistical techniques are used).

During the audit, consider whether any errors detected require amendments in the nature, timing or extent of audit tests.

Consider the materiality impact of the previous period's unadjusted errors on the current year's results.

Obtain audit partner approval for the level of unadjusted misstatements. The auditor may have to request the directors to amend the entity's financial statements, if material.

# SAS 230
## *Working papers*

**Issued March 1995**

**Summary**
Sets out standards required for the content of working papers and the period for which these should be retained.

**Key Points**

Document all material matters of principle and judgement met during the audit to provide a record of the relevant facts on which the audit opinion was based.

Audit working papers should document:
- Planning and performance
- Supervision and review
- Evidence supporting the auditor's opinion.

Working papers are the property of the auditors and should be retained for at least six years (longer if they may be required).

Working papers should be kept confidential.

To provide audit evidence, working papers should record:
- What audit procedures were undertaken
- When they were undertaken
- By whom
- The reviewer's name and date.

## Application Notes

Standardised working papers often help in ensuring the efficiency of the audit and in controlling the quality. Beware, however, of a stereotyped approach to audits.

Check that any schedules prepared by the client are correct.

Ensure that all working papers:

- State an objective
- Provide evidence of the work done, when and by whom
- Show what conclusion was reached
- Are approved by the reviewer (for example, manager/partner).

Keep working papers for a period of at least six years. Details of acquisitions of fixed assets, goodwill on the acquisition of an entity, etc. may need to be kept longer – consider putting these in the permanent audit file.

Before destruction of audit files, confirm that they are unlikely to be required in the future.

Maintain the following files (where appropriate) separately:

- Taxation
- Secretarial
- Audit (permanent and annual)
- Permanent financial statements
- Special engagements.

Update working papers to resolve any matters arising out of the review of the audit by the partner/manager.

Update permanent audit file where necessary (for example, new loan agreements or share/group structure changes).

Ensure safe custody of working papers during and after audit. Obtain audit partner approval for external access to files.

# SAS 240
## *Quality control for audit work*

**Issued March 1995**

### Summary
Sets out the standards required in quality control both in the audit firm and the individual audit engagement.

### Key Points
Establish quality control policies for the firm, to ensure that all audits are conducted in accordance with SASs.

Policies should include:
- Professional requirements
- Skills and competence required
- Not accepting (or retaining) clients that cannot be serviced properly
- Assignment of work and supervision requirements
- Consultation
- Monitoring of standards.

For each audit, the audit partner must apply the firm's policies taking into account the requirements of the specific audit.

The audit partner is responsible for ensuring that work carried out by the firm's staff can be relied upon in reaching the audit conclusion – the audit must be planned, supervised and reviewed.

The normal requirements are:
- Audit plan (background of business; possible auditing and accounting problems, and extent of testing required)

- Time budgets
- Competent staff for the job
- Supervision
- A review (to ensure tests are completed as planned, documented correctly and that conclusions are consistent with the test results).

## Application Notes

Establish and document quality control policies and procedures to ensure all audit assignments are performed in accordance with SASs.

Communicate quality control policies and procedures to all staff.

Inform staff of changes in quality control policies and procedures.

Ensure the technical and professional competence of staff. Send staff on relevant courses to make aware them of updates in technical pronouncements.

Ensure that only staff with appropriate levels of skill, competence and experience are assigned to tasks.

Ensure that all work performed is adequately planned, directed, supervised, documented and reviewed.

Perform regular reviews of existing clients to confirm the appropriateness of the firm continuing to serve as auditor.

Evaluate prospective clients prior to accepting the engagement.

Monitor on an independent basis the effectiveness of the operation of quality control policies and procedures. Select a number of audits each year for review by another partner (if possible).

# SAS 300

## *Accounting and internal control systems and audit risk assessments*

**Issued March 1995**

**Summary**

Sets out the standards required in assessing audit risk, developing audit programmes to reduce the risk to an acceptable level, and the necessity of understanding the accounting and internal control systems in use.

**Key Points**

There are three components in audit risk:

- Inherent risk: Risk of error or misstatement, assuming no internal controls
- Control risk: Risk of error or misstatement not prevented or detected by internal controls or accounting systems
- Detection risk: Risk that audit tests of transactions, balances, and analytical procedures will not detect a material error or misstatement.

Assess audit risk using professional judgement. Then design procedures to reduce to an acceptable (low) level of risk.

Understand the entity's accounting and internal control procedures – note that auditors are only concerned with controls relating to financial statement assertions (see SAS 400).

Inherent risk assessment is based on the experience of previous audits plus an evaluation of factors at financial statement, account balance and class of transactions levels.

Evaluate the effectiveness of the company's internal control systems in detecting and preventing errors or misstatements (preliminary assessment).

Plan tests of controls to reduce the levels of substantive tests. If the preliminary assessment is not supported by the results of the tests of the internal controls, modify the substantive tests accordingly.

Ensure that evidence is obtained that no changes have occurred in the internal control system, if relying on interim audit tests.

Perform some substantive procedures for all material account balances and transaction balances (analytical procedures may suffice in some cases).

The higher the risk, the greater the need to obtain more audit evidence.

If the risk cannot be reduced to acceptable levels, consider the audit report implications – perhaps even consider withdrawal from the audit.

In businesses where little segregation of duty is possible, it is likely that auditors will perform only substantive tests to obtain audit evidence and therefore will not need to evaluate or test internal control systems.

## Application Notes

Assign audit staff with appropriate levels of skill, knowledge and experience to assess audit risk.

Document the accounting system (flowcharts are easier to understand – and update – than written compositions!).

Document the internal control system (the procedures being used by management to achieve the proper conduct of the business).

Assess the effectiveness of the system in identifying material errors in the financial statements. Plan the audit procedures accordingly.

To assess audit risk, examine the following areas:

- Items in the financial statements that are difficult to estimate (for example, contract work-in-progress valuation, or bad debts provision)
- Unusual transactions and journal entries (particularly near year end)
- Complex transactions, where the substance of the transactions are not easy to understand
- Assets that are easily misappropriated
- Involvement of related parties with the entity
- Extremely tight deadlines for reporting (soon after the year end) that increase the risk of error
- Profit-related bonuses for management
- Pressure to match budgets or profit forecasts
- Changes in key personnel during the period.

Design the planning approach to be taken (see SAS 200).

Perform substantive testing on all major items in the financial statements, even if the risk is assessed as low.

Increase the amount of substantive testing where internal controls are not assessed as effective – for many small clients, substantive tests only will be the norm.

Where reliance on controls is planned, confirm the effective operation of controls throughout the period by testing a sample of transactions. Consider whether there were any changes in the accounting or internal control systems during the financial period. Assess whether the results of tests confirm the initial risk assessment – if not, consider appropriate action.

Inform management of any weaknesses noted in either the accounting or internal control systems (see SAS 610).

# SAS 400
# *Audit evidence*

**Issued March 1995**

## Summary

Gives guidance on the procedures recommended to obtain audit evidence and establishes standards for the quantity and quality of evidence required.

## Key Points

Obtain sufficient audit evidence to make reasonable conclusions in forming the audit opinion.

If appropriate evidence cannot be obtained, consider the implications for the audit report.

Check:
- The design of the internal control system
- That the system has operated effectively during the period (this applies if seeking audit evidence from testing the internal control systems).

The evidence from substantive tests undertaken should support the financial statement assertions.

Assertions are the explicit or implied representations by management embodied in financial statements. Normally audit evidence is required to support each financial statement assertions, which are:
- Existence: The asset or liability exists at a given date
- Rights and obligations: The asset or liability pertains to the entity

- Occurrence: A transaction or event pertaining to the entity has taken place during the period
- Completeness: No unrecorded assets, liabilities, transactions or events or no undisclosed items
- Valuation: Asset or liability is carried at an appropriate carrying value
- Measurement: A transaction or event is recorded at the proper amount and revenue or expense is allocated to the proper period
- Presentation and disclosure: An item is disclosed classified and described in accordance with applicable legislation and accounting standards.

Audit evidence is obtained by one or more of the following procedures:
- Inspection
- Observation
- Enquiry and confirmation
- Computation
- Analytical procedures.

Substantive tests are of two types:
- Tests of details of transactions and balances
- Analytical procedures.

## Application Notes

Test (and document) all major balance sheet and profit and loss figures by inspection, observation, enquiry, confirmation, and computation.

For less material items and transactions, use analytical procedures.

Report to management any weaknesses noted in tests of the accounting and/or internal control systems.

Obtain external evidence (for example, confirmation from the entity's solicitor) about the existence of litigation, acquisition or disposal of assets rather than internal evidence.

Obtain, where possible, confirmations of major items (for example, debtors and bank confirmations) directly to the auditor's offices.

List material oral representations, for which no documentary evidence is available, so that these can be included in management's letter of representation.

Consider the implications for the audit report of insufficient evidence.

Revise the audit programme, where appropriate, in the light of results of tests of the accounting and internal control systems, analytical review procedures and substantive tests.

Obtain audit evidence up to the date of the audit report (SAS 150).

Consider contingencies and possible illegal acts.

Confirm compliance with laws and regulations (SAS 120).

Consider the use of computer aided audit techniques (CAAT).

Investigate audit differences and prepare a summary of unadjusted differences.

# SAS 410
# *Analytical procedures*

**Issued March 1995**

## Summary

Gives guidance and establishes standards as to when analytical procedures should be used during an audit.

## Key Points

Analytical procedures should be applied both at the planning stage (to identify areas of potential risk) and the overall review stage (to ensure the financial statements are consistent with the conclusions arrived at) of an audit.

Analytical procedures involve the analysis of significant ratios and trends in the business and the investigation of fluctuations or deviations from expected patterns.

Analytical procedures can be used on their own as a substantive procedure for audit evidence – normally for items that are not material.

Investigate significant fluctuations or deviations from expected patterns – obtain explanations and other supporting evidence.

If no explanations are available (or are inadequate), decide on extra audit procedures to be undertaken to ascertain the reason for the fluctuation or deviation.

## Application Notes

For each client, build up a 'Key ratios/figures' profile and keep this on the permanent audit file.

The profile could include, for instance:

- Turnover (by product, geographical area, major customers)
- Gross profit (by product, geographical area)
- Sales commission
- Bad debts
- Payroll costs
- Major costs of production
- Employee numbers
- Net assets
- Stock turnover
- Market share.

Analyse the key ratios of the entity at the planning stage of the audit. Compare to previous years and against budget. Compare with similar entities, if information is available.

Consider the use of the computer as a tool to assist in developing analytical procedures.

Use non-financial information where available (for example, production quantities adjusted for stock movements to verify total sales volume) in addition to financial data.

Discuss with management the reasons for any unusual deviations from previous years or from expected results. Assess the implications of the discussions for planning audit procedures.

Consider whether the data analysed is relevant and reliable – test controls over the preparation of data.

At or near the end of the audit, perform appropriate analytical procedures to confirm that the original analysis was valid and that the financial statements are consistent with the auditor's knowledge and understanding of the business.

# SAS 420
# *Audit of accounting estimates*

**Issued March 1995**


## Summary
Gives guidance on, and sets standards for, the audit of accounting estimates made by management, that are included in financial statements.


## Key Points
Auditors are likely to exercise more judgement when examining accounting estimates as evidence supporting same is generally more persuasive than conclusive.

Accounting estimates normally include amounts relating to:
- Net realisable value and obsolescence of stock
- Depreciation
- Deferred taxation
- Outcome of legal cases pending
- Construction work-in-progress
- Provisions for warranties
- Amortisation period of development costs.

To audit an accounting estimate, the auditor should do at least one of the following:
- Examine how management arrived at the estimate
- Obtain an independent estimate
- Review subsequent events that support the estimate made.

Assess the reasonableness of each estimate in the light of other evidence obtained during the audit and the auditor's knowledge of the business (and ensure adequate disclosure if appropriate).

Towards the end of the audit, assess the reasonableness of all accounting estimates for the period together to ensure that the sum of the reasonable differences are not biased in one direction.

## Application Notes

At the audit planning stage, assess the risks in accounting estimates that may result in a material misstatement in the financial statements.

Discuss with management the policies and procedures in place for the timely identification and correct accounting for accounting estimates. Report any weaknesses noted and suggest improvements.

Consider skills, competence and experience of company staff responsible for preparing the accounting estimates.

Compare prior period accounting estimates with actual results for accuracy. Check that differences are properly accounted for.

Consider the assumptions underlying the calculation of the accounting estimates.

Test the calculations of the accounting estimates.

Consider the accuracy and completeness of the data used in the calculation of accounting estimates.

Consider management approval for the accounting estimates (include in the letter of representation).

Perform an appropriate subsequent events review to assess the accuracy of the accounting estimates (see SAS 150).

Consider the use of independent expertise, where appropriate.

Tests for usual accounting estimates may include:

- Stock obsolescence: Obtain aged listing of stock (physical inspection can sometimes suffice). Compare this with normal stock turnover for each product
- Net realisable value: Check post year end sales values for major products
- Depreciation: Compare to previous year; check calculations on new additions; check sample of items fully depreciated (ask whether any of these still in use)
- Warranties: Examine sales documentation to see whether warranties have been given; compare actual result for the year against the previous estimate; consider the appropriateness of the accounting policy, if long-term warranties are given
- Deferred taxation: Obtain capital expenditure plans and check directors' meetings for evidence of approval; consider the effect if projects are delayed
- Legal cases: Obtain a letter from the entity's solicitor setting out details of any legal cases pending, together with likely outcomes
- Construction work-in-progress: Obtain assessments from the entity's architects as to likely final outcome of each project and any known potential risks.

# SAS 430
# *Audit sampling*

**Issued March 1995**


### Summary
Sets out the standards required when using sampling techniques to select items that can be evaluated for audit evidence and applying the conclusions reached to the whole population from which the items have been selected.


### Key Points
Audit sampling involves selecting less than 100 per cent of items within an account balance or class of transactions, performing tests and using the results to form a conclusion regarding the rest of the items.

If statistical sampling is used, mathematically constructed conclusions can be reached from the results whereas if non-statistical sampling is used the auditor's opinion is based on judgement alone.

Consider the sampling risk, allowable error and expected error when deciding on the sample size.

Compare the conclusion that would be reached if the entire population was tested as against the conclusion reached from testing the sample – this is the 'sampling risk'.

The allowable error is the maximum auditors will accept without changing their opinion – if the allowable error is to be small, a large sample is needed.

If errors are expected, select a sufficiently large sample to ensure that the actual error is less than the expected error.

In sampling, ensure that all items in the population being tested have an opportunity of being picked.

Sampling methods in normal use are:

- Random (using random number tables)
- Systematic (constant interval after a random start)
- Haphazard (may be difficult to ensure an unbiased sample).

Analyse the errors found – consider their nature, cause and possible effect on other aspects of the audit.

Project the errors found to the population tested – re-assess the sampling risk. If risk has increased too much, perform other audit procedures (the result may be an adjustment to the financial statements).

## Application Notes

At the audit planning stage, consider the use of sampling techniques as an audit tool. This is most likely to be effective where:

- There is a large number of insignificant items
- The population consists mainly of routine transactions
- It has been decided to adopt a substantive audit approach.

At the outset, specify the audit objectives to be achieved through sampling.

Confirm that the population sample is appropriate to achieve the specified audit objective.

Consider different sampling techniques, selecting one that ensures the sample is representative of the population.

Avoid haphazard selection of samples (where possible).

Use systematic or random number tables, which assume all items in the population have equal chance of selection.

Stratify the population where appropriate – for example, confirm all debtor balances over £x and a small sample of those under £x.

Define the conditions that constitute an error.

If some errors are expected, make the sample size big enough so that the errors found will be representative of the population.

Evaluate sample results – consider the level of errors found and project this across the entire population using a basis of projection consistent with the basis of the sample selection.

Take the probable overall error to the error summary sheet (see SAS 220) – not just the errors found.

Extend the tests if a common cause of errors is seen – concentrate on just the problem area.

Re-assess the sampling risk if the projected error exceeds the allowable error. If the risk is unacceptable, consider extending the audit procedures or performing alternative audit procedures.

# SAS 440
# *Management representations*

**Issued March 1995**

### Summary
Sets standards for evaluation, documentation and use of important representations made by management during an audit.

### Key Points
The directors are responsible for the financial statements – the auditor should obtain evidence that the directors acknowledge this responsibility.

Acceptable audit evidence includes minutes of board meetings, a written letter or a signed copy of the financial statements incorporating a statement of directors' responsibility.

Representations from management on material matters in financial statements are often necessary for audit evidence – obtain these in writing.

Management representations are **not** a substitute for other audit evidence where this is available.

Investigate the reason if audit evidence casts doubt on management representations (Which is incorrect? Was there a misunderstanding? What is the effect on the audit?).

Where written representations on an important matter are not given by management, this constitutes a limitation of scope in audit. Can the auditor rely on other representations? Consider the effect on the audit report.

## Application Notes

Instead of a separate letter, the signatures of the directors on the directors' report and on the statement of directors' responsibilities will be sufficient evidence of the directors' approval of the accounts and their acknowledgement of responsibilities.

Set out the responsibilities of the directors in the letter of engagement.

During the audit, list all material representations received where no other audit evidence was available, and include these in the letter of representation.

In a group situation, obtain letters of representation regarding both the group accounts and the parent company.

Investigate the reasons for any discrepancy between representations made by management and other evidence obtained during the audit.

If management will not sign the letter of representation, consider the implications for the audit report (limitation of scope). Consider why the directors will not sign.

The date of the letter of representation should be the same day as the audit report approval, if feasible (or as near to that date as is possible).

Items that may need to be included in management's letter of representation:

- Details of guarantees, etc.. issued by the entity
- Basis of research and development costs deferred
- Stocks – valuation/risk of obsolescence
- Contract work-in-progress – directors not aware of any unforeseen costs
- Basis of deferred taxation
- Details of 'related parties' of the entity

- Directors' view of the outcome of legal cases pending
- Doubtful debts provision
- Capital expenditure commitments
- Valuation of unquoted investments
- Compliance with laws and regulations
- All material oral representations made during the audit.

Note: The letter of representation should include only items where the matters of fact are confined solely to management or areas that involve significant levels of directors' estimates/judgement.

# SAS 450
# *Opening balances and comparatives*

**Issued March 1995**

## Summary

Sets out, in the context of both recurring audits and first year engagements, the necessity to ensure the opening balance sheet figures and comparatives are correctly stated.

## Key Points

Compare the opening balances in nominal ledger to the closing balance of the preceding period – these must agree, unless there have been prior year adjustments or accounting policy changes.

Make sure there are no material errors in opening balances – if comparatives are adjusted for material errors, disclosure must be made.

Account for, and disclose, any changes in accounting policies.

If previous years' statements were qualified and the matter is:

| | |
|---|---|
| **Still unresolved** | Qualify with regard to opening balances and comparatives |
| **Still unresolved but does not affect opening balances** | Qualify with regard to comparatives |
| **Resolved** | Give an explanation of how treated |

Incoming auditors assume audit responsibility for comparatives – review last year's accounts, compare them with the current period and the comparatives.

If the comparatives have not been audited, disclose this clearly.

Consultations with previous auditors are normally held only to obtain clarification of significant accounting matters.

If the accounts have been qualified by previous auditors, pay special attention to the area qualified.

## Application Notes

Agree the opening trial balance to last year's balance sheet.

Review the journal entries made at the start of the financial year.

Check that the accounting policies have not altered – if altered, ensure the comparatives are changed to reflect each new policy and that proper disclosure is made in the financial statements.

Consider the appropriateness of any change in the accounting policies.

Check that any matters qualified in last year's audit report are properly treated (see **Key Points**).

Review the current year's financial statements to ensure that the previous years' audited figures correctly disclosed. Disclose any restatement/regrouping of comparative figures.

Ensure adequate disclosure in the financial statements if the comparatives are unaudited. Consider implications for audit report.

Consider, in the current year, whether the previous year's figures are free from material misstatement (for example, review the outcome of material prior year accounting estimates – see SAS 420).

Ensure the correct and adequate disclosure of any amendment to comparatives required due to subsequent material error being discovered/noted.

# SAS 460 (draft)
## *Related parties*

**Issued December 1994**

### Summary
Provides guidance on the audit of related party transactions and their disclosure in financial statements.

### Key Points
Directors are obliged to disclose transactions with related parties.

A related party can be an individual group of individuals, a partnership or other business entity where there is an ability to influence (or be influenced) directly or indirectly the operations of the reporting entity. (Family members of key management of the entity and its parent are also assumed to be related parties.)

Auditors should design audit procedures to ensure all material related party transactions are identified and adequately disclosed in the financial statements.

Assess the risk of unidentified material related party transactions.

Obtain written representations from the directors confirming full disclosure of related party transactions and, where applicable, the controlling party (and ultimate controlling party).

Consider the implications for the audit report if disclosure is inadequate or sufficient audit evidence is not available.

## Application Notes

At the audit planning stage, obtain a list (in writing) from the management of related parties. Keep this in the permanent audit file and update each year.

Design procedures to check the recording of transactions with related parties (Is such recording part of the normal accounting system or a special 'once-off' analysis?).

Check/review the related party disclosures of transactions for the current reporting period. Obtain appropriate audit evidence.

Consider whether there are other transactions not reported. Be aware of transactions with extended terms of credit, unusual terms of trade, etc..

Ensure that the audit staff inform the audit partner if they become aware of any material related party transaction(s) not among the transactions listed by the directors.

Ensure that auditors of foreign components of the entity are aware of the requirements of this SAS. Provide details of known related party transactions to the auditors concerned.

Ensure that appropriate reference to related party transactions and disclosures are included in the letter of representation.

# SAS 470
# *Overall review of financial statements*

**Issued March 1995**

## Summary

Sets out the standards required to be met by auditors in making a final review of the financial statements before signing the audit report.

## Key Points

At the end of an audit, auditors must review the financial statements, and the audit evidence obtained, to ensure there is a reasonable basis for their audit opinion.

Ensure the financial statements comply with accounting standards and company law requirements.

Ensure the financial statements are consistent with other information and with the results of the audit opinion reached on the basis of audit testing.

## Application Notes

Assign the task of overall review of the financial statements to a person with an appropriate level of knowledge and experience.

Allow sufficient time for review before the sign-off deadline.

Use a company accounts checklist each year – retain it on the audit file, duly signed off by the appropriate staff and audit partner. Ensure that the checklist contains the latest Financial Reporting Standards requirements.

Use a checklist to ensure support for financial statements is complete – retain it on file. The checklist will normally include the following:

- Support/evidence of profit and loss account and balance sheet items (including analytical review)
- Company accounts checklist (as previously mentioned)
- Subsequent events review
- Commitments and contingencies review
- Solicitors' letters and experts' reports
- Extracts from minutes – shareholders, directors, audit committee or management meetings
- Lease commitments
- Complex transactions – substance over form review
- Insurance review
- Reports to management/directors/audit committee – and response
- Consideration of laws and regulations applying to entity
- Review of directors' report and other information
- Directors' emoluments , loans, options
- Pension scheme review
- Related parties information/disclosure
- Going concern period evaluation.

Review the accounts package (including 'other information' being sent to shareholders) to ensure there is adequate disclosure of material items.

Confirm that the accounting policies are appropriate and are consistently applied.

Agree any amendments to the financial statements with management, the directors, or the audit committee (as appropriate).

Consider whether items included in management's letter of representation are adequately disclosed, where necessary, in the financial statements.

Consider whether the analytical procedures (SAS 410) disclose any information that may affect the presentation or disclosure of items in the financial statements.

# SAS 500
## *Considering the work of internal audit*

**Issued March 1995**


### Summary
Sets out the standards required when considering using work done by a client's internal audit function to assist in planning the audit.


### Key Points
External auditors have sole responsibility for the audit opinion expressed on a set of financial statements.

Work carried out by internal auditors may be useful to external auditors but the auditor must realise that the objectives of internal audit are determined by management and are different from the external auditors' objectives.

Assess the effectiveness of internal audit work where relevant to external audit.

Criteria:

- Internal audit status in entity (any constraints placed on internal audit activity?)
- Scope of function – management action on recommendations
- Technical competence of audit team
- Internal control planning, supervision, review and documentation.

Evaluate any specific internal audit work (this may involve testing to ensure it is adequate) used to reduce extent of external audit work.

If not adequate, revise tests planned to obtain sufficient evidence to support audit conclusion.

## Application Notes

At the planning stage, make a preliminary assessment of whether the use of the internal audit function can assist in the audit, by reducing the amount of testing required.

Agree with management, the directors or audit committee (as appropriate) the use of the internal audit function for the purpose of the external audit.

Meet with the internal audit manager and assess the internal audit function.

Examine the scope of the internal audit team, their experience, the documentation and reports issued.

Obtain copies of internal audit reports – review actions taken by management subsequent to the reports.

Agree in advance with the internal auditors the tests, documentation and sampling methods to be undertaken and the timing thereof.

Supervise internal audit staff and review their work, where relied upon.

If, after review, the internal audit work is deemed to be inadequate, decide what extra tests or evidence are required to meet the audit objectives.

Liaise with the internal audit function at regular intervals during the year.

Consider using the internal audit function to assess procedures not directly impacting on the financial statements (for example, compliance with, and monitoring of, laws and regulations affecting the entity).

# SAS 510
# *The relationship between principal auditors and other auditors*

**Issued March 1995**

## Summary

Sets out the standards applicable where one or more components included in the financial statements of an entity are audited by other auditors.

## Key Points

Principal auditors must ensure that the work carried out by other auditors provides sufficient audit evidence.

Auditors should only accept the position of principal auditor if satisfied that their participation is sufficient to give a proper audit opinion.

Check that the other auditors are professionally qualified to undertake the audit of the component(s).

Check that the other auditors' procedures are adequate – (for example, questionnaires/checklists, review of working papers.

Discuss significant findings of other auditors both with the other auditors and with the management of the component.

Other auditors are responsible for the audit opinion on the component they are auditing. They should co-operate with, and assist the principal auditor (they may have to obtain permission from the component's management to communicate with the principal auditor – if this is refused, they must notify the principal auditor).

Principal auditors have sole responsibility for their audit opinion.

Do not refer to other auditors in the audit opinion. However, if a component's audit report is qualified, it may be necessary for the principal auditor to reflect that fact in his or her audit report.

The Companies Act (s.389A, UK; s. 397, Northern Ireland; s.196, Republic of Ireland) imposes a duty on a subsidiary and its auditors to give information and explanations reasonably required to the principal auditor to enable him or her to carry out his or her duties as the auditor of the holding company.

## Application Notes

Consider, as principal auditor:

- The materiality of the components audited by other auditors
- The competency of the other auditors, the adequacy of their knowledge of the business and their independence – obtain written confirmation at an early stage.

Decide whether it is appropriate to act as principal auditor.

If acting as principal auditor, ensure the letter of engagement makes clear to the directors of the entity their responsibilities regarding the group financial statements.

Set out in the letter of engagement what information the auditors of components should notify (and when) to the principal auditor.

Agree at the planning stage, for each component:

- The material areas that need special attention
- Reporting requirements for inter-group transactions and related party transactions
- Timetable for audit completion
- Contact names.

Review other auditors' working papers – the more material the component, the more regular the review.

Obtain and review a written summary of the other auditors' procedures and findings. Confirm compliance with requirements set out in the planning correspondence.

Assess the impact of the other auditors' findings on the group audit.

Arrange for the other auditors to submit copies of the managements' letters of representation (SAS 440) and their reports to management (SAS 610) with the financial statements of the components they audit.

Update the permanent audit file – knowledge of the business section – with any relevant information.

Make special arrangements to obtain the co-operation of auditors of components of the entity that are not subsidiaries – for example, joint ventures, associated companies, quasi-subsidiaries.

# SAS 520
# *Using the work of an expert*

**Issued March 1995**


## Summary
Sets out the standards required if using the work of an expert to obtain audit evidence.


## Key Points
Auditors are not expected to have the expertise of a person qualified in another profession or occupation (for example, an actuary or engineer).

Ensure that the independence, objectivity and integrity of the auditors is not affected if the 'expert' engaged for an assignment is employed by them or is associated with them.

To determine whether the use of an expert is needed, consider:
- Whether the matter is material
- The risk of error or misstatement in financial statements
- The quantity and quality of other audit evidence.

If auditors need to use experts, discuss with management – if management is unable or unwilling, look for other audit evidence that may be available .

Ensure that the expert chosen is professionally competent and objective.

Review the expert's terms of reference to ensure that the scope of work is adequate to provide appropriate audit evidence

Review the expert's findings and ensure that (if auditor is happy) these are properly disclosed in financial statements or that they support the financial statement assertions.

If there is inconsistency between other audit evidence and the results of the expert's work, attempt to resolve the inconsistency by discussing it with the entity's management and the expert.

## Application Notes

At the planning stage determine what, if any, of the financial statement assertions require to be evidenced by specialists ('experts') such as actuaries, architects, lawyers, valuers, surveyors, engineers etc.

Agree with management the most appropriate expert, who must preferably be independent of the entity. If management is not willing, consider whether this constitutes a limitation of audit scope.

Confirm the integrity, objectivity, and professional competence of the expert.

Set out, with management, the terms of reference for the expert:

- What evidence is needed
- The purpose of the report
- Whether the report (or extracts) will be published or referred to
- Assumptions, bases to be used (ensure consistency with previous reports).
- Timing of the work.

If management has already engaged the expert, request a meeting to explain the audit objective to the expert and obtain confirmation that the expert's report is useful for audit purposes.

Confirm that the expert has had adequate access to all data and information necessary for the purpose of the report.

Obtain and review the expert's report and consider the implications for the audit – consider whether the results are consistent with other audit evidence.

Do not refer to the work of the expert in the audit report if accepting the work as valid audit evidence. Consider whether appropriate disclosure of the expert's work is required in the financial statements.

# SAS 600
# *Auditors' reports on financial statements*

**Issued May 1993**

## Summary

Establishes standards and gives guidance on the form and content of audit reports issued on financial statements.

## Key Points

The audit report is the final product of the audit of the financial statements of an entity. In completing the audit, ensure that all the following aspects have been considered (and documented!):

- Responsibility
- Planning, controlling and recording
- Accounting systems and internal control
- Evidence
- Using the work of others.

The audit report must give a clear expression of opinion, based on an assessment of the evidence obtained.

The report must:

- Identify those to whom it is addressed – for example, the shareholders of ABC Limited
- Identify which statements are being reported on – for example, the historical cost statements (as modified by the revaluation of certain fixed assets) for the year ended (date)

- Set out the responsibilities of the directors – unless these are adequately covered in another part of the financial statements or accompanying information
- Set out the responsibilities of the auditor, including an explanation of what constitutes an audit – testing, assessing estimates, checking accounting policies, and disclosure and presentation of information. Also the fact that the audit was planned so as to obtain all information and sufficient evidence to ensure the financial statements are free from material misstatement
- Explain the basis of the audit opinion
- Give the audit opinion – only refer to the profit and loss account and balance sheet (there is no requirement to report on other statements)
- Contain the signature (written or typed) of the auditor
- Be dated.

*Fundamental uncertainty*
If a fundamental uncertainty is adequately accounted for and properly disclosed, include an explanatory paragraph but **no** qualification.

*Limitation of audit scope*
Where the auditor is unable to get enough evidence to reach an unqualified opinion:

- He or she must describe the limitation
- If its effect is material, issue a disclaimer of opinion
- If its effect is not material, qualify and explain possible adjustments.

*Disagreement on accounting treatment or disclosure*
Describe, give implications and quantify (where possible) the effect and:

- If the financial accounts are misleading, give an adverse opinion
- For other material items, qualify using an 'except for' paragraph.

*Signing and dating of audit report*
To be done only after the financial statements, directors' report, etc. have been approved by the directors and the package reviewed by the auditor. (Normally only a short interval should elapse between board approval and audit signature; if a long period elapses, the auditor must ensure the accounts are still approved.)

## Example of an unqualified audit report – UK company

***Auditors' report to the shareholders of ABC Limited***

*We have audited the financial statements on pages 5 to 18 which have been prepared under the historical cost convention (as modified by the revaluation of certain fixed assets) and the accounting policies set out on page 5.*

*Respective responsibilities of directors and auditors:*
*As described on page 3 the company's directors are responsible for the preparation of financial statements. It is our responsibility to form an independent opinion, based on our audit, on those statements and to report our opinion to you.*

*Basis of opinion:*
*We conducted our audit in accordance with Auditing Standards issued by the Auditing Practices Board. An audit includes examination, on a test basis, of evidence relevant to the amounts and disclosures in the financial statements. It also includes an assessment of the significant estimates and judgements made by the directors in the preparation of the financial statements, and of whether the accounting policies are appropriate to the company's circumstances, consistently applied and adequately disclosed.*

*We planned and performed our audit so as to obtain all the information and explanations which we considered necessary in order to provide us with sufficient evidence to give reasonable assurance that the financial statements are free from material misstatement, whether caused by fraud or other irregularity or error. In forming our opinion we also evaluated the overall adequacy of the presentation of information in the financial statements.*

*Opinion:*
*In our opinion the financial statements give a true and fair view of the state of the company's affairs as at 31 December 1994 and of its profit for the year then ended and have been properly prepared in accordance with the Companies Act 1985.*

*U No Who &Co.*
*Registered Auditors*
*Blank Street.*
*1 March 1995*

In the Republic of Ireland the opinion section would read:
*In our opinion the financial statements give a true and fair view of the state of the company's affairs as at 31 December 1994 and of its profit for the year then ended and have been properly prepared in accordance with the Companies Acts 1963 to 1990.*

*We have obtained all the information and explanations we consider necessary for the purposes of our audit. In our opinion, proper books of account have been kept by the company. The financial statements are in agreement with the books of account.*

*In our opinion, the information given in the directors' report on page 2 is consistent with the financial statements.*

*The net assets of the company, as stated in the balance sheet on page 7, are more than half of the amount of its called up share capital and, in our opinion, on that basis there did not exist at 31 December 1994 a financial situation which, under section 40(1) of the Companies (Amendment) Act 1983, would require the convening of an extraordinary general meeting of the company.*

## Statement of directors' responsibilities – example for a large UK company

If this is not presented separately in the financial statements, it must be included in the second paragraph of the audit opinion:

*Company law requires the directors to prepare financial statements for each financial year that give a true and fair view of the state of affairs of the company and of the profit or loss of the company for that period. In preparing those financial statements, the directors are required to:*

- *Select suitable accounting policies and then apply them consistently*
- *Make judgements and estimates that are reasonable and prudent*
- *State whether applicable accounting standards have been followed, subject to any material departures disclosed and explained in the financial statements (large companies only)*
- *Prepare the financial statements on the going concern basis unless it is inappropriate to presume that the company will continue in business.*

*The directors are responsible for keeping proper accounting records that disclose with reasonable accuracy at any time the financial position of the company and to enable them to ensure that the financial statements comply with the Companies Act 1985. They are also responsible for safeguarding the assets of the company and hence for taking reasonable steps for the prevention and detection of fraud and other irregularities.*

## Application Notes

The audit partner must review the audit file and ensure that the support for the financial statements checklist (see SAS 470) is complete.

Summarise the important points of the financial statements and the entity's business.

Review the summary of unadjusted audit differences.

Consider the appropriateness of the going concern 'foreseeable future' period chosen as regards additional disclosure (if less than one year) and whether a longer period is necessary.

Check that a letter of representation and a statement of directors' responsibilities are obtained.

Discuss with management, the directors, and audit committee (as appropriate) the basis of the audit opinion (see **Key Points**). Confirm that no unusual matters have occurred or arisen since the audit work was completed.

Agree with management, the directors, and audit committee (as appropriate) whether extra audit evidence can be obtained to overcome the limitation (if any) of audit scope.

Inform management, the directors, and audit committee (as appropriate) of any changes required in accounting treatment or disclosure in the financial statements to avoid qualification or a disclaimer of opinion.

Explain the reasons for the wording of the audit report and notes in the financial statements if there is a 'fundamental uncertainty' consideration.

Obtain the directors' approval of (minuted), and signatures to, the financial statements package.

Issue the audit report, date it and sign as Registered Auditor.

# SAS 610
# *Reports to directors or management*

**Issued March 1995**


## Summary
Sets out the requirements regarding the reporting of weaknesses, in both accounting and other internal control systems, to directors and management.


## Key Points
A report is an important result of an audit.

Report material weaknesses identified in the accounting and internal control systems and suggest improvements.

Suggest improvements in efficiency identified during the audit.

Comment on errors (whether adjusted or not) and particular accounting policies and practices that appear to be inappropriate.

A letter or report to management cannot excuse a qualification where this is required by SAS 600.

Normally address the letter or report to management to the board of directors or the audit committee. Request a reply showing actions, if any, to be taken by directors.

Make the report immediately after completion of audit.

Consider the audit implications of matters raised in previous reports.

Make sure permission is received from management of subsidiaries before informing the parent entity's management of contents of management reports relating to the relevant subsidiary.

To reduce liability to a third party, state in the report that:
- It was prepared for entity's use
- Permission is required before it may be disclosed to anyone else
- No responsibility is accepted towards any person other than the addressee(s) of the report.

## Application Notes
During the audit, note all matters that should be brought to the attention of management, the directors or audit committee (as appropriate).

Address the report to the level appropriate in the entity – that is, those who can act on the points raised.

Report (and suggest improvements) on failures and weaknesses identified in the accounting and internal control systems.

Comment on the appropriateness of the accounting policies followed.

Comment on the implications of foreseeable accounting or legislative changes.

Matters raised should include references to description of observations, suggested improvements and the benefit of action by the management.

Suggest improvements in other (non-financial) areas identified during the audit.

Reports should be constructive and timely. Consider reporting after the interim audit and again after the year end audit.

Follow up matters raised in previous reports and include them in the current year's report, where appropriate.

Request a response from management.

The report should explicitly state:

- That it is not comprehensive and excludes items that may arise from a special review
- That the report is for the entity and should not be distributed to third parties without prior consent.

Do not issue a copy of the report other than to the entity (unless permission is given).

# SAS 620

# *The auditors' right and duty to report to regulators in the financial sector*

**Issued March 1994**


### Summary

Sets out standards to be met by auditors of businesses in the financial sector to fulfil their statutory duty to report to regulators in certain circumstances.


### Key Points

Legal requirements to report to regulator are set out in:

*UK*

- Building Societies Act 1986
- Banking Act 1987
- Financial Services Act 1986
- Insurance Companies Act 1982
- Friendly Societies Act 1992

Note: Statutory Instruments set out the duty to report under the above Acts.

*Ireland*

- Building Societies Act 1989
- Central Bank Act 1989
- Trustees Savings Bank Act 1989
- Insurance Act 1989
- European Communities (UCITS) Regulations 1989
- Unit Trust Act 1990

- ACC Bank Act 1992
- ICC Bank Act 1992
- Companies Act 1990 (section 258).

In addition to reporting on financial statements, auditors have extra reporting responsibilities to regulators under the above acts.

Where the auditor becomes aware, during the course of the audit, of certain information, a report is required by the regulator on matters specified by law or regulation (statutory responsibility).

Notify the appropriate regulator as soon as possible where there is a responsibility to report and if the matter is likely to be of significance to the regulator.

Normally agree the report with the directors but note that statutory responsibility takes precedence over the auditor's duty to the entity.

If the matter casts doubt on the integrity of the directors, the auditor should report directly to the regulator (without informing the directors). The duty to report does not mean that the auditor must carry out specific work; report only if the matter arises as part of normal audit procedures.

The contents of a report might include:

- The name of the entity
- The statutory ower under which the report is made
- The fact that the report is made in accordance with SAS 620
- Context
- Subject matter
- Auditor's signature and date of report
- A request for confirmation of receipt.

Planning, supervision and control of audits of regulated bodies should be performed in a manner similar to other audits (the knowledge level of the special rules etc. applying must be high – for example, the scope of the entity's authorisation).

Where there are matters arising, not covered by rules of reporting, but which are important, initially request the directors to notify the regulator; if this is not done, the auditor should notify the regulator.

When drafting the audit opinion on the financial statements, consider the effect of matters notified to the regulator.

The statutory responsibility to report information to regulators relates to information obtained in the course of the audit. Information or knowledge obtained in other capacities may not normally be disclosed, as it would breach the duty of confidence.

## Application Notes

Maintain on the permanent audit file a copy of relevant legislation applicable to the client.

Maintain on the permanent audit file a copy of the relevant APB Practice Note (relating to banks, building societies, investment businesses, insurance companies and friendly societies, as appropriate).

Ensure all audit staff are aware of the contents of legislation and Practice Note(s) applicable to each client.

Ensure all audit staff immediately notify the audit partner of any breach in regulations noted. Consider whether the breach is of material significance to the regulator (duty to report direct without delay) or not significant (right to report direct).

Note: Material significance to the regulator may not be material in relation to the financial statements.

Design procedures within the firm to ensure that the audit partner is informed of any non-audit work undertaken for a regulated client and considers the results of this non-audit work when planning (and reviewing) the audit.

# Auditing standards and the smaller company

Auditing standards are intended to be applied to all audits of financial statements (unless there is a specific exemption in a standard).

## Audit exemptions

In Ireland, the Company Law Reform Commission recommended that companies with a turnover under £100,000 should be exempt from the audit requirement. In March 1995, a commitment to implement this recommendation was given by the government, though no date was set for legislation.

From 1994, companies in the UK that meet the criteria below are exempt from the audit requirement:

- Balance sheet total less than £1,400,000
- Turnover less than £90,000.

Exemption from audit can only be blocked if shareholder(s) holding 10 per cent or more of the shares of the company deposit a notice in writing at the company's registered office at least one month prior to the financial year end requesting an audit.

Companies whose balance sheet total is less than £1,400,000 but whose turnover is between £90,000 and £350,000 (if a charity, £250,000) can opt for an accountant's report. This option is not available to plcs, group companies, banks, or insurance companies, regardless of their qualification on balance sheet or turnover grounds.

## The accountant's report

This report must be prepared by a suitably qualified accountant (who need not be a registered auditor).

The reporting accountant must give his or her opinion on three matters:

- Whether the accounts are in agreement with the accounting records
- Whether, having regard only to, and on the basis of, the information contained in the accounting records, the accounts have been drawn up in a manner consistent with the accounting requirements specified in the Companies Act 1985
- Whether the company has satisfied the conditions for exemption from an audit as specified in the regulations.

In the event that the accounts are not in agreement with the accounting records or not drawn up in accordance with the legislation, the reporting accountant must qualify his or her opinion.

The reporting accountant does not perform an audit – that is, no verification of turnover or balance sheet totals is required nor must independent evidence be obtained to support the figures in the financial statements.

Directors of companies that avail of the audit exemption must state in the financial statements that:

- The company is eligible to take advantage of the audit exemption
- They are aware of their obligation to keep proper records and to prepare accounts that give a true and fair view of the company's position.

This is in addition to the usual statement of directors' responsibilities included in the financial statements.

# Statement of Standards for Reporting Accountants
## *Audit Exemption Reports*

**Issued October 1994**
**Effective UK only, for reports signed on or after 21 December 1994**


### Summary
Sets out the standards required of accountants reporting on accounts of small companies exempted from the statutory audit requirement but whose turnover is in excess of £90,000 and less than £350,000 (except in the case of a charity, where the gross income limit is £250,000).


### Key Points
The report must be prepared by a suitably qualified accountant (who need not be a registered auditor).

A letter of engagement is necessary.

Prepare and document a work programme.

Direct, supervise and review work done by assistants.

Working papers should evidence work done and record and support the conclusions reached.

Check that the accounts are in agreement with the accounting records – if not, qualify the report.

Check that the accounts have been prepared in accordance with the accounting requirements specified in section 249C(6) of the Companies Act 1985 – if not, qualify the report.

If a limitation is put on the scope of the work, qualify the report.

Do not issue a report if the company is not entitled to exemption from the audit or if unable to reach a conclusion on this. Notify the directors.

Resign from the engagement if the accounts are misleading (and this cannot be dealt with adequately in the report).

## Application Notes

All clients in this category must receive a new letter of engagement – otherwise there will be confusion about exactly what work is being undertaken. Ensure all existing engagement letters are superseded or withdrawn.

Do not carry out an audit – that is, do not look for original documents, independent evidence, bank confirmations, debtors confirmations, title deeds etc.

If the reporting accountant has prepared the financial statements, they should be in agreement with the books of account – otherwise check a number of entries from the nominal ledger through to the final accounts.

Check that the company is exempt from audit – that is:

- Balance sheet totals less than £1,400,000
- Turnover less than £350,000 (if a charity, £250,000)
- The company was not at any time during the year:
  > A public company
  > A banking or insurance company
  > Listed under the Insurance Brokers (Registration ) Act 1977
  > An authorised person (or appointed representative) under the Financial Services Act 1986
  > An employer association or trade union
  > A member of a group.

Use a Companies Act checklist.

Set out details of the accounting records.

Ensure that work delegated to assistants is reviewed and supervised (and evidenced).

Ensure that the financial statements include a statement by the directors that:

- The company is entitled to avail of the audit exemption
- The members (or those of them holding 10 per cent or more of the issued share capital) have not requested an audit
- Notes the requirements to keep proper records and to prepare accounts giving a true and fair view.

## Example of accountant's report with unqualified opinion

***Accountant's Report to the Shareholders on the unaudited accounts of ABC Limited***

I report on the accounts for the year ended 31 December 1994 set out on pages 3 to 14.

*Respective responsibilities of directors and reporting accountant*
As described on page 2, the company's directors are responsible for the preparation of the accounts, and they consider that the company is exempt from an audit. It is my responsibility to carry out procedures to enable me to report my opinion.

*Basis of opinion*
My work was conducted in accordance with the Statement of Standards for Reporting Accountants and so my procedures consisted of comparing the accounts with the accounting records kept by the company, and making such limited en-

quiries of the officers of the company as I considered necessary for the purposes of this report. These procedures provide only the assurance expressed in my opinion.

*Opinion*

In my opinion:

(a) The accounts are in agreement with those accounting records kept by the company under section 221 of the Companies Act 1985

(b) Having regard only to, and on the basis of, the information contained in those accounting records,
(i) the accounts have been drawn up in a manner consistent with the accounting requirements specified in section 249C(6) of the Act, and
(ii) the company satisfied the conditions for exemption from an audit of the accounts for the year specified in section 249A(4) of the Act and did not, at any time within the year, fall within any of the categories of companies not entitled to the exemption specified in section 249B(1).

*U NO WHO*
*Reporting Accountant*
*Blank Street*
*1 March 1995*

From the example, the following requirements are evident:

- Name(s) of those to whom it is addressed
- Which statements are being reported on
- Responsibilities of the directors set out
- Basis of the opinion explained
- Opinion given
- Name and signature of the reporting accountant
- Date.

# Also published by Oak Tree Press

**Accounting Standards: A quick reference**
**Second edition**
**Niall MacLochlainn and Brian O'Kane**

Accounting standards for the UK and Ireland are set by the Accounting Standards Board, an independent body which, since its formation in 1990, has issued seven Financial Reporting Standards and adopted more than 20 Statements of Standard Accounting Practice issued by its predecessor, the Accounting Standards Committee. Also in issue are more than a dozen exposure drafts and other documents issued for discussion and consultation.

This revised and updated edition summarises all the standards and documents in force as of 31 December 1994, using clear straightforward language. It will prove invaluable for student and practitioner alike.

**132 pages; paperback; £9.95**
**ISBN 1-872853-84-6**